idea book

a creative idea book
for the
elementary teacher

written and illustrated
by
Karen Sevaly

poems by
Margaret Bolz

Copyright © 1990, 2001
Teacher's Friend, a Scholastic Company.
www.teachersfriend.com
All rights reserved.
Printed in China.

ISBN-13 978-0-439-49961-3
ISBN-10 0-439-49961-5

Table of Contents

This book is dedicated to teachers and children everywhere!

Notes:

Let's Make It!

Let's Make It!

Children are especially responsive to the various holidays and themes associated with the four seasons. With this in mind, Teacher's Friend has published the "Winter" Idea Book to assist teachers in motivating students.

WHO USES THIS BOOK:

Preschool and elementary teachers along with scout leaders, Sunday school teachers and parents all love the monthly and seasonal idea books. Each idea or craft can easily be adapted to fit a wide range of abilities and grade levels. Kindergartners can color and cut out the simple, bold patterns while older students love expanding these same patterns to a more complex format. Most of the ideas and activities are open-ended. Teachers may add their own curriculum appropriate for the grade level they teach. Young children may practice number, color or letter recognition while older students may like to drill multiplication facts or match homophones.

WHAT YOU'LL FIND IN THIS BOOK:

Teachers and parents will find a variety of crafts, activities, bulletin board ideas and patterns that complement the monthly holidays and seasonal themes. Children will be delighted with the booklet cover, bingo cards, nametags, mobiles, place cards, writing pages and game boards. There is also a special section devoted to the sport of the season!

HOW TO USE THIS BOOK:

Every page of this book may be duplicated for individual classroom use. Some pages are meant to be used as duplicating masters or student worksheets. Most of the crafts and patterns may be copied onto construction paper or printed on index paper. Children can then make the crafts by coloring them using crayons or colored markers and cutting them out. Many of the pages can be enlarged with an overhead or opaque projector. The patterns can then be used for door displays, bulletin boards or murals.

Making mobiles is especially fun for all ages. Teachers may like to simplify mobile construction for young children by using one of these ideas.

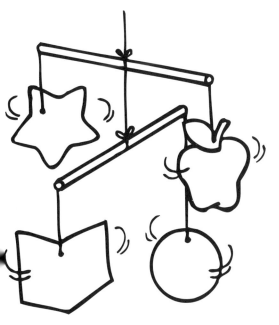

DRINKING STRAW MOBILE

Thread a piece of yarn through a plastic drinking straw and tie a mobile pattern to each end. Flatten a paper clip and bend it around the center of the straw for hanging. The mobile can easily be balanced by adjusting the yarn. (Older students can make their mobiles the same way but may wish to add additional levels by hanging other mobiles directly below the first.)

CLOTHES HANGER MOBILE

Mobiles can easily be made with a wire clothes hanger, as shown. Just tie each pattern piece to the hanger with thread, yarn or kite string.

YARN MOBILE

Gluing the pattern pieces to a length of yarn makes the most simple mobile, each piece spaced directly beneath the other. Tie a bow at the top and hang in a window or from the ceiling.

CLIP ART PAGES:

The illustrations on these pages may be used in classroom bulletins, newsletters, notes home or just to decorate your own worksheets. Copy the clip art pages, cut out the illustrations you want, and paste them to your original before printing. The drawings may be enlarged or reduced on a copy machine. You are also free to enlarge the illustrations for other uses, such as bulletin boards, calendar decorations, booklet covers and awards.

PLACE CARDS OR NAMETAGS:

If possible, laminate the finished nametags or place cards after you have copied them onto colored index paper. Use a dry transfer marker or dark crayon to write each name on the laminated surface. After the special day, simply wipe off the names with a tissue for use at another time.

POETRY:

Children love simple, clever poetry. Use the poems in this book to inspire your students. You may want to have the students rewrite the poems for a timely record of their advancing handwriting skills.

Each morning, copy one or two lines, or an entire poem, on the class board. Ask the children to copy it in their best handwriting. Instruct them to write the date at the top of the page. Collect the poem pages and organize them chronologically in individual folders. This is a great way to show parents how their child's handwriting has improved throughout the year.

STAND-UP CHARACTERS:

All of the stand-up characters in this book can easily be made from construction or index paper. Children can add the color and cut them out. The characters can be used as table decorations, name cards or used in a puppet show. Several characters can also be joined at the hands, as shown. The characters can also be enlarged on poster board for a bulletin board display or reduced in size for use in a diorama or as finger puppets.

BULLETIN BOARDS:

Creating clever bulletin boards can be a fun experience for you and your students. Many of the bulletin board ideas in this book contain patterns that the students can make themselves. You simply need to cover the board with bright paper and display the appropriate heading. Students can make their own stocking for a classroom Christmas mantle or creative writing mittens for a fun winter display.

Many of the illustrations in this book can also be enlarged and displayed on a bulletin board. Use an overhead or opaque projector to do your enlargements. When you enlarge a character, think BIG! Figures three, four or even five feet tall can make a dramatic display. Use colored butcher paper for large displays eliminating the need to add color with markers or crayons.

WHATEVER YOU DO...

Have fun using the ideas in this book. Be creative! Develop your own ideas and adapt the patterns and crafts to fit your own curriculum. By using your imagination, you will be encouraging your students to be more creative. A creative classroom is a fun classroom! One that promotes an enthusiasm for learning!

WINTER

WINTER ACTIVITIES

SNOWMAN SEQUENCE

WINTER BULLETIN BOARDS

MR. SNOWMAN

JACK FROST

WINTER MOBILE

CREATIVE WRITING MITTENS

WINTER ACTIVITIES!

CATCH A SNOWFLAKE!
The next time it snows, have your students run outside and catch snowflakes on pieces of dark colored construction paper. Ask them to examine the snowflakes carefully and see if there are any two snowflakes alike. (For best results, keep the construction paper in a refrigerator so that the snowflakes melt more slowly.)

WINTER IMPROVISATIONS!
Ask your students to act out the life of a snowflake. The children will love pantomiming the forming of the snowflake, floating to the ground and eventually melting.

FREEZING WATERS
Winter is a great time of year to teach children what happens to water when it freezes!

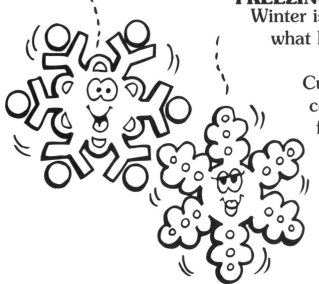

Cut the top off a large tin can and fill it completely with water. Place the can in the freezer or outside overnight, if your weather is cold enough. The next morning, ask students to examine the level of the water.

Older children may like to research the reasons why some substances contract while others expand when frozen.

This would be a great time to make frozen Popsicles that the whole class can enjoy.

ABOUT THE SEASONS

What is the real reason
That we have each season?

When it's WINTER and it rains and snows,
We bundle up like Eskimos.

Flowers and blossoms cover the ground
When winter is finished and SPRING comes around.

We readily know it's SUMMER we've got
When the temperature's high and the sun is hot.

Then AUTUMN comes when the weather is chilly,
When cold, crisp winds blow willy-nilly.

There are these seasons, numbering four.
When all are finished, they repeat once more.

WINTER BINGO!

This game offers an exciting way to introduce students to the winter season.
Give each child a copy of the bingo words listed below or write the words on
the chalkboard. Ask students to write any 24 words on his or her bingo card.
Use the same directions you might use for regular bingo.

WINTER BINGO WORDS

WINTER	SLED	STOCKINGS	SHADOW
COLD	SKIS	REINDEER	LINCOLN
FREEZE	SLOPES	HANUKKAH	WASHINGTON
SNOW	DECEMBER	CANDLES	VALENTINE
ICE	JANUARY	NEW YEAR	HEARTS
ICICLE	FEBRUARY	MIDNIGHT	CUPID
MITTENS	CHRISTMAS	RESOLUTION	LOVE
JACKET	HOLIDAY	CELEBRATION	FLOWERS
GIFTS	SNOWFLAKE	MARTIN LUTHER KING, JR.	CANDY
SANTA	SNOWMAN	GROUNDHOG	LEAP YEAR

WINTER BINGO

FREE

WINTER NEWS!
A NOTE HOME TO PARENTS!

SNOWMAN SEQUENCE CARDS!

WINTER BULLETIN BOARDS!

WINTER MONITORS

Liven up that old monitor bulletin board with a new winter theme. Display a large snowflake in the middle of the board and label each branch of the snowflake with a classroom job. Children's names can be written on smaller snowflakes or strips of paper and placed next to each job. Rotate the names during winter months. You can also use this idea to note reading or math groups.

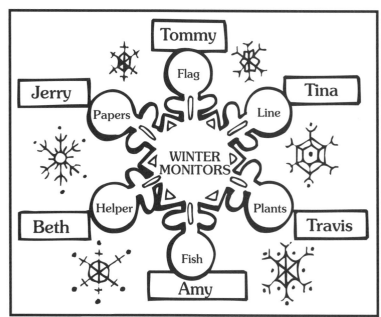

CHILLY REPORTS

Display a winter weather character off to the side of your class bulletin board. Students can write reports about their winter weather observations. The reports can be shown on the board with paper icicles hanging from each one. The title "Chilly Reports" can be cut from white Styrofoam trays for a three-dimensional effect.

CLASSY SNOWPEOPLE

Children will love making and then displaying look-a-like snowpeople. Have each student cut out a large white paper snowman. Ask them to draw in the features to resemble themselves. They may like to add items which depict their interests or hobbies. Line the snowpeople up along a class bulletin board and ask students to guess who's who.

Winter Weather Character

Snowflake Pattern

19

Mister Snowman!

Cut this Mister Snowman from index paper. Add your own original snowman face, color, cut out and fold. Attach his hat to his left hand with a brass fastener.

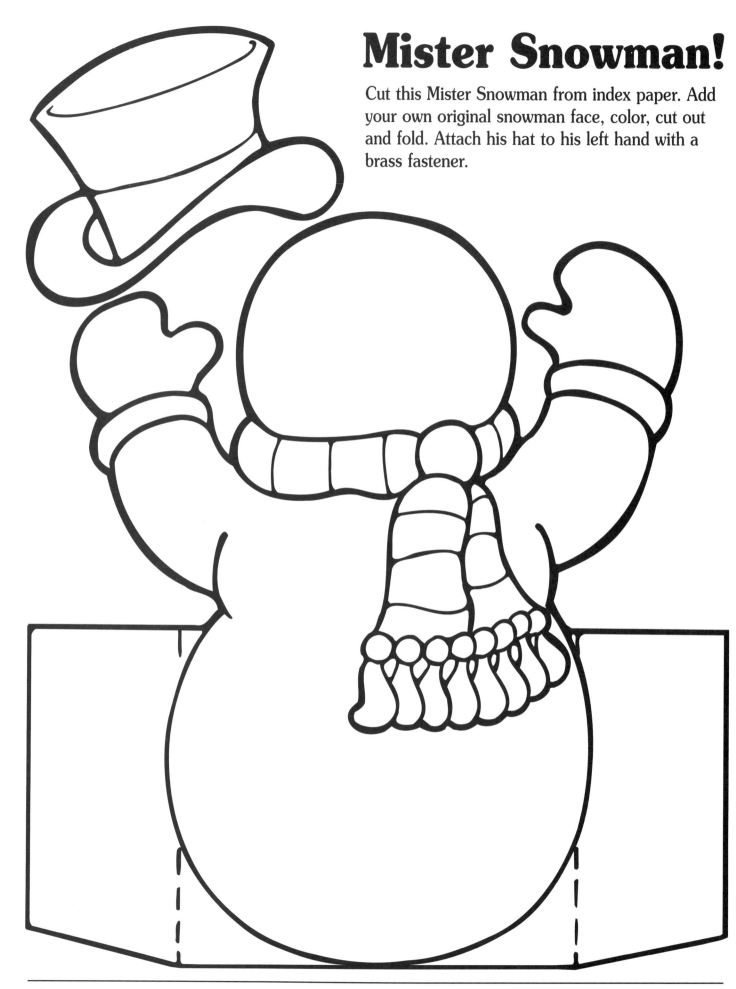

Matching Snowmen!

Make several copies of snowmen and hats from colored construction paper. Use them in a variety of matching activities such as letter recognition, math facts, opposites, vocabulary words and definitions and so on.

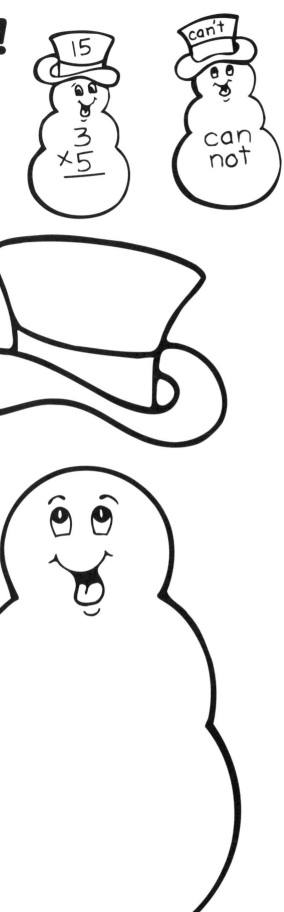

Jack Frost!

Jack Frost is an imaginary elf that supposedly creates the lacy patterns of frost on windows, trees, and just about everything in the cold, winter outdoors.

He's found in countless nursery rhymes and children's stories, often nipping people's noses with the cold. Jack Frost is often said to appear only after we have gone to sleep. He then darts from window to window, painting lacy crystals or frost on each pane.

Children might like to write creative stories about Jack Frost, or descriptive poems after observing Jack's beautiful icy creations.

Cut this Jack Frost from colored paper. Color with markers or crayons. Use brass fasteners to assemble at the dots.

Teachers: You might like to award one pattern piece of Jack Frost for each act of good behavior or completed assignment. Children can then assemble the pieces together when they have collected all six pieces.

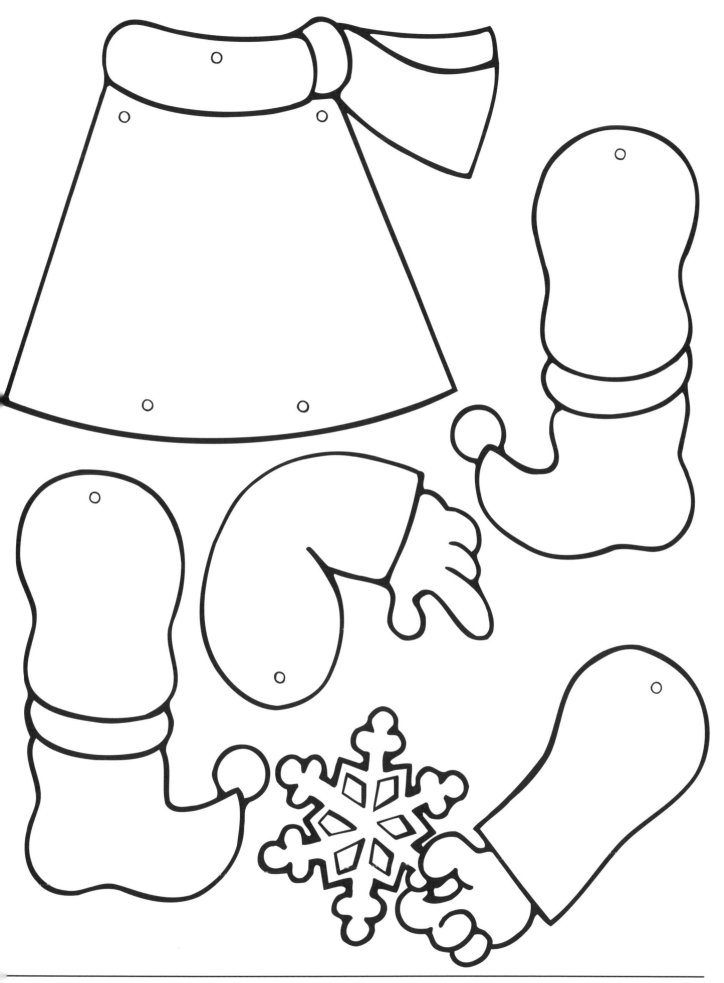

Winter
Mobile

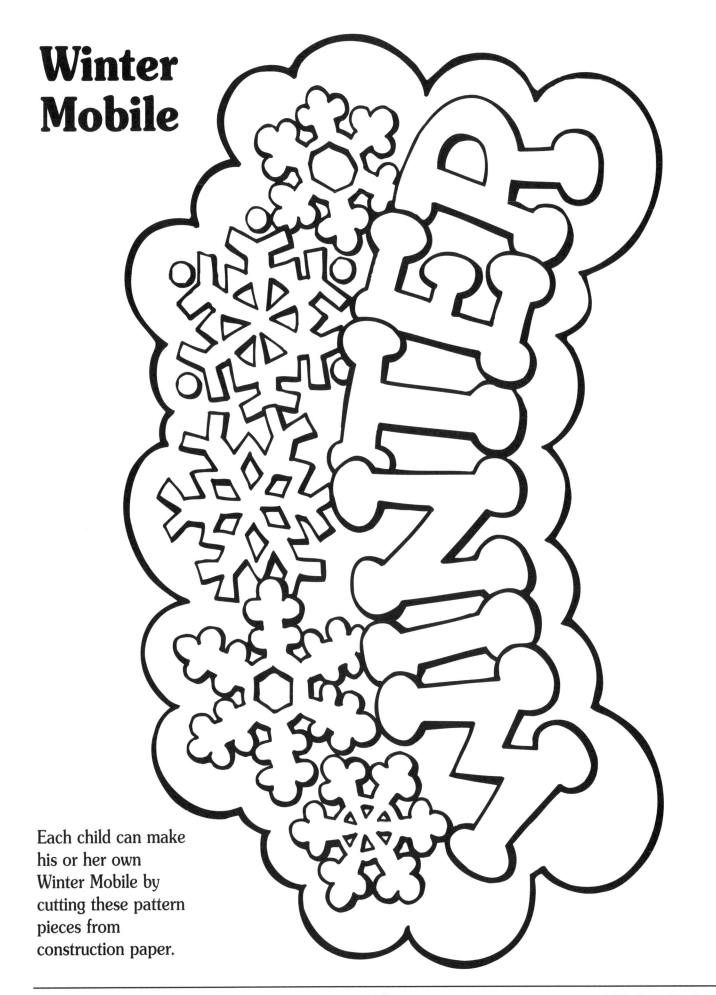

Each child can make
his or her own
Winter Mobile by
cutting these pattern
pieces from
construction paper.

24

Hang with kite string or heavy
thread.

These snowflake patterns can
also be used as winter
nametags or bulletin board
decorations.

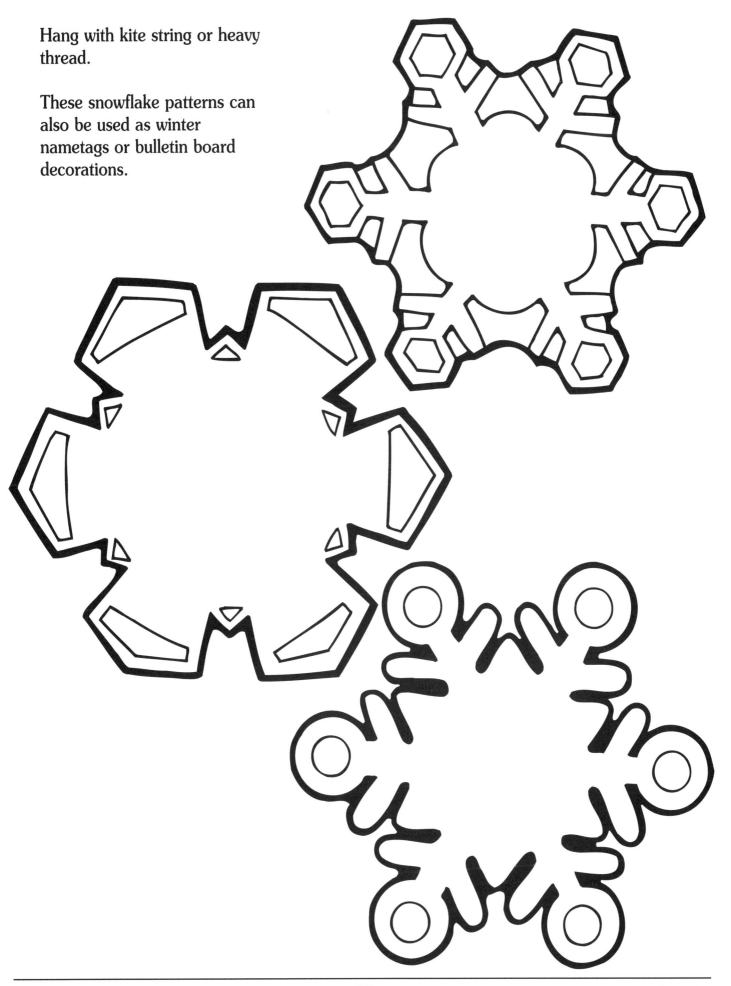

Creative Writing Mittens!

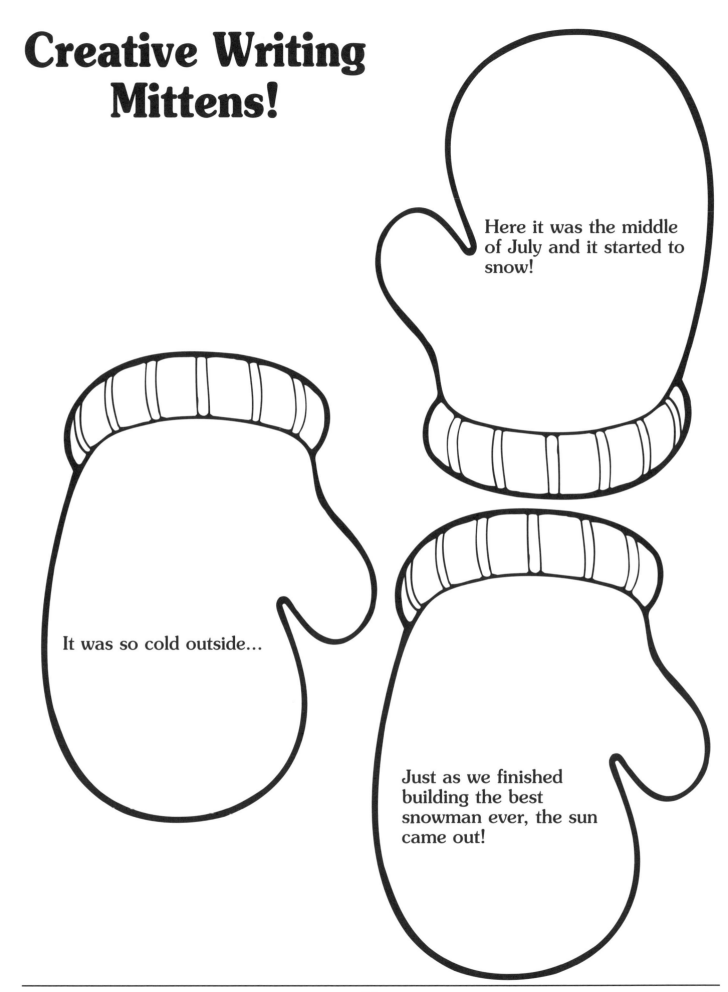

Here it was the middle of July and it started to snow!

It was so cold outside...

Just as we finished building the best snowman ever, the sun came out!

 TF1602 Winter Idea Book

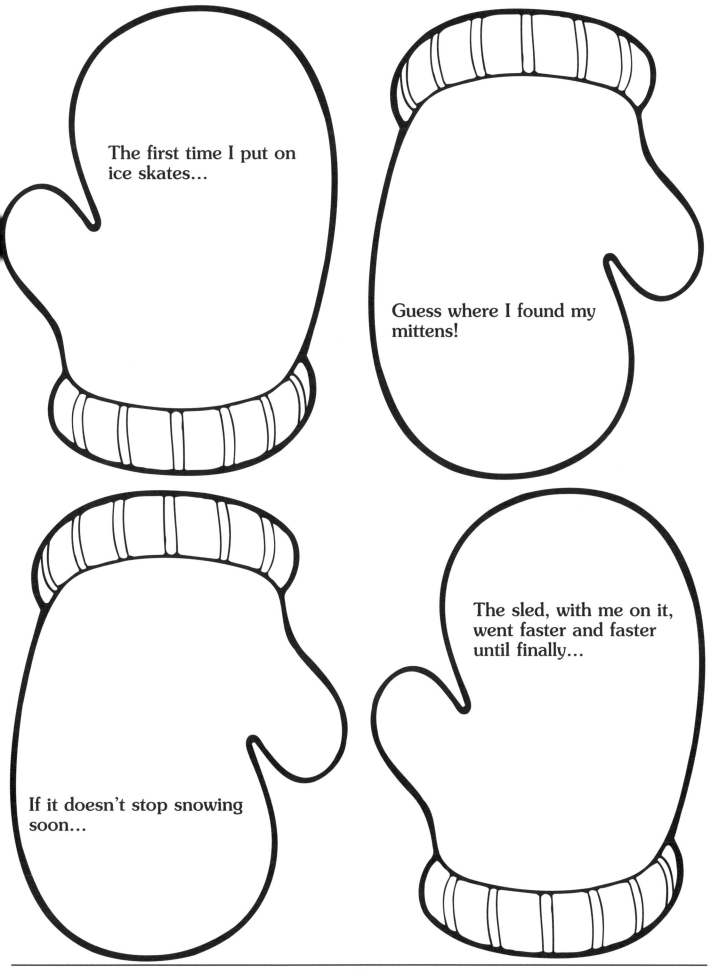

The first time I put on ice skates...

Guess where I found my mittens!

If it doesn't stop snowing soon...

The sled, with me on it, went faster and faster until finally...

TF1602 Winter Idea Book

My Mitten Story!

Name

DECEMBER

DECEMBER CLIP ART
DECEMBER AWARDS
DECEMBER ACTIVITIES
SANTA SEQUENCE CARDS
DECEMBER BULLETIN BOARDS
SANTA CHARACTER
STAND-UP SLEIGH AND REINDEER
MANGER MOBILE

GINGERBREAD MEN
DECEMBER FUN GLASSES

GIFTS FOR MOM AND DAD
MY HANUKKAH BOOK

December Clip Art

DECEMBER NEWSLETTER!

TEACHER:	RM#	DATE:

Type the name of your
school, address and
telephone number
in this space.

SUGGESTIONS FOR A DECEMBER NEWSLETTER:

- List the name of each student that was selected student of the week for the month of November.

- Note the dates of Christmas vacation. Make sure that parents know which days children will not be in attendance.

- Announce special holiday programs or plays being conducted by your school or in your classroom.

- Ask one of your students to draw several small pictures about Christmas or Hanukkah to be used as clip art.

- Ask your school principal to write a brief message that can be included with the December newsletter.

- Ask for parent volunteers or donations for the class holiday party and/or class food drive.

- Staple the December cafeteria menu to each newsletter.

- Send a welcome note to a new student or a get-well message to a student that has been out ill.

- Suggest to parents that they encourage their children to read or catch up on incompleted schoolwork during the holiday vacation.

- Wish your students and their families a happy holiday and a wonderful new year!

- Tell about something special your class is currently working on.

SUPER STUDENT AWARD!

awarded to

_____

for

_____

_____

_____

_____

Date

_____

Teacher

December

STUDENT OF THE MONTH

AWARDED TO

_____
Name

_____

_____ _____
Teacher   Date

DECEMBER ACTIVITIES!

DECEMBER
Winter begins when fall is done
About December twenty-one.
Our family sings with happy voices
Christmas songs; the world rejoices.
Christmas means a holly wreath
And Christmas tree with gifts beneath.
One week later is New Year's Eve.
Old Father Time is sure to leave.
At the stroke of twelve, you will hear
People shouting, "Happy New Year!"

'TWAS THE NIGHT BEFORE CHRISTMAS...
Do you need a simple classroom skit for the holidays? Try this easy, but fun idea!

Assign one set of the lines from the poem "A Visit From St. Nicholas" by Clement Moore, to each student in class. Ask the students to illustrate their section of the poem on a large sheet of construction paper. They should also memorize their section of the poem.

On skit day, have each student take his or her turn reciting the lines of the poems and holding up the corresponding pictures. Instruct the entire class to recite the last line together, "Happy Christmas to all, and to all a good night!"

Display the student-made illustrations on the class bulletin board for a clever holiday mural.

Candy Cane Rudolph
Twist two pipe cleaners around the top of a small cellophane-wrapped candy cane for Rudolph's antlers. Glue two small buttons for eyes and a red pompom for his nose. Hang Rudolph on the tree as a holiday ornament or give him to a friend as a special treat.

SANTA SEQUENCE CARDS!

DECEMBER BULLETIN BOARDS!

STOCKING STUFFERS

Have your students stuff a large Christmas stocking for an easy holiday bulletin board.

Have each child write his or her name on a strip of construction paper. Ask them to cut pictures from magazines, to represent what they would like for Christmas, and glue them to strips of construction paper. Students might like to make individual stockings that can be pinned to a paper fireplace mantel displayed on the class bulletin board.

CLASS CHOIR

Have each student draw his or her own portrait on a white, fluted, paper plate. Ask them each to draw his or her mouth in a singing position. Attach a white collar and a red bow to the chin of each face. Arrange the faces on the class bulletin board to display your class choir.

HOLIDAY DREAMS

Children can draw self-portraits that are then tucked into a bulletin board quilt. (Make the quilt from old wallpaper samples.)

Place a white paper cloud above the children's heads and have students write or draw in their holiday dreams.

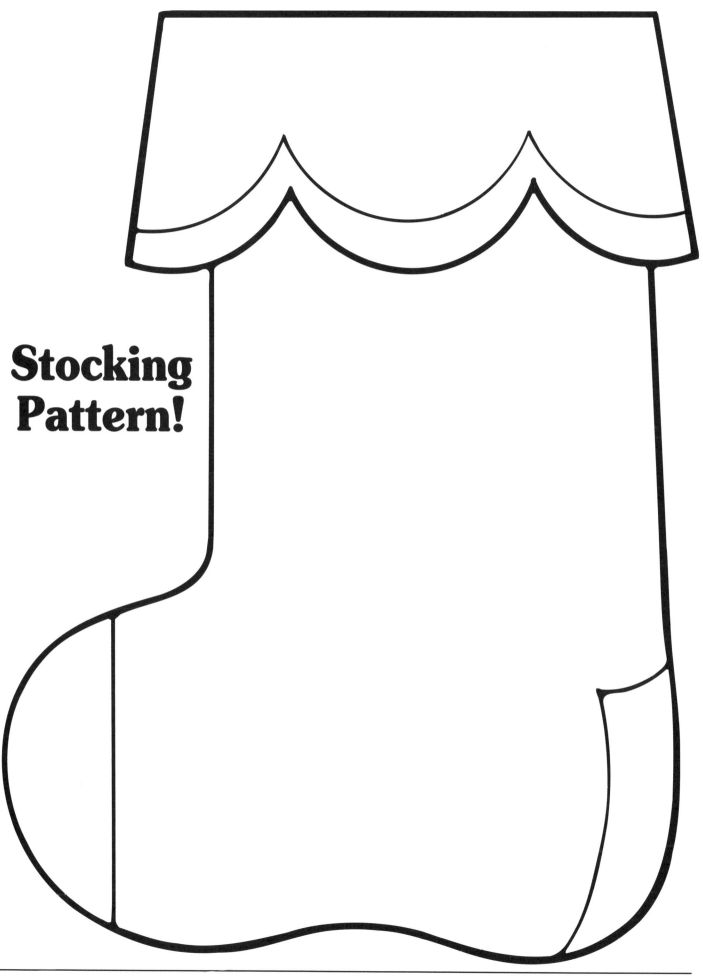

Stocking Pattern!

Santa Character!

Cut this Santa character from index paper. Color, cut and fold. Stand him on a table for a special Christmas decoration.

Stand-Up Reindeer!

Cut this reindeer pattern from index or construction paper. Fold along the dotted line to make him stand up.

Stand-Up Sleigh!

Color with markers and decorate with glitter. Punch out the small circles with a hole punch. Cut four, four-inch sections from plastic drinking straws. Insert the straw sections into the holes, as shown, to make the sleigh stand up. Display the sleigh on a table top with three or four standing reindeer.

Stand-Up Holiday Gifts!

Cut out the wreath and gifts from heavy paper. Write your own holiday message on the gifts. Fan-fold along the dotted lines. Glue the wreath to the first gift and stand on a desk top for a festive decoration.

TF1602 Winter Idea Book

Gingerbread Men!

Gingerbread men are fun to make and so good to eat!

Trace and cut out the gingerbread man pattern below onto cardboard. Use a packaged gingerbread mix and follow the directions on the box for rolled gingerbread cookies. Have the children roll the dough onto waxed paper and trace around the cardboard pattern using a rounded, plastic knife. Have the students place raisins for eyes and cinnamon red-hots for the mouth. After baking, white frosting can be applied to outline clothes and to add buttons.

Children will enjoy following the directions and helping with the cleanup when the reward is a freshly baked gingerbread cookie!

GINGERBREAD MEN ORNAMENTS

These gingerbread men ornaments will smell like the real thing!

Make these simple, paper ornaments from brown construction paper or a large, heavy grocery bag. Instruct the children to trace the pattern and cut him out. Use a spray adhesive to the front of each gingerbread man and sprinkle him with powdered cinnamon or ginger. The students can then decorate the gingerbread men with white poster paint using a small brush. When dry, attach a thread to the top of each head and hang them on a Christmas tree.

Gingerbread House Greeting Card!

Copy this gingerbread house pattern onto construction paper, color and cut out.

Fold the front of the card to the center and write a holiday message inside.

Gingerbread Man Booklet!

Ask students to write "yummy" stories or holiday recipes inside this gingerbread man booklet. He can also be used as a holiday card to send to friends!

December Fun Glasses!

Cut the pattern pieces from heavy index paper and color with markers or crayons. Attach the bows to the frame by fitting them into the designated slots.

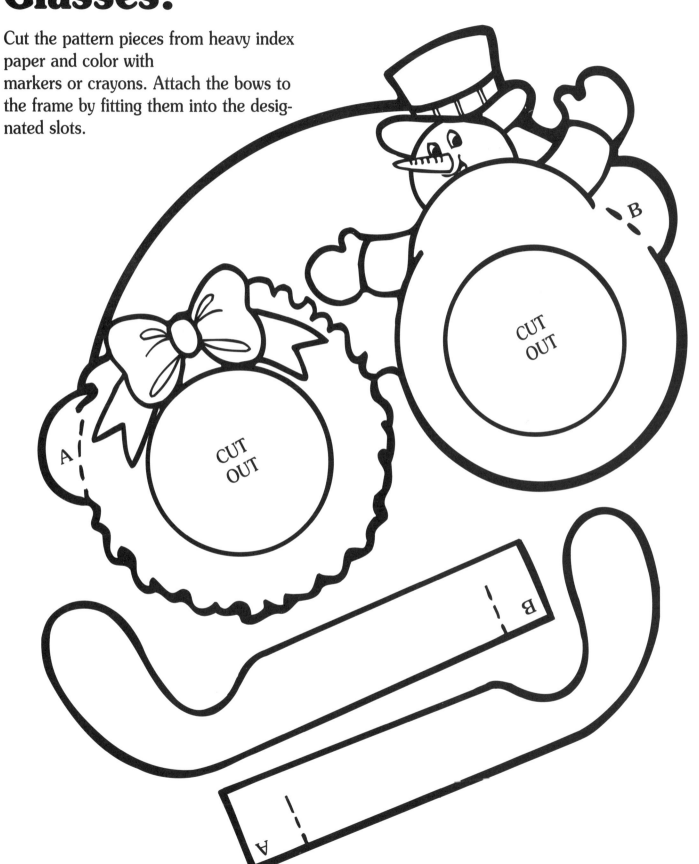

My Wish List!

Holiday Writing!

Manger Mobile!

Glue the angel to the top of the manger before attaching the string.

Each student can make his or her own "Manger Mobile" using these simple patterns. Cut the patterns from index or construction paper and assemble with thread or yarn, as shown.

Handy Coin Holder!

Give Dad a "handy" coin holder as a holiday gift!

Cut two hand patterns from colored felt. Stitch or glue the edges of the hands together. Glue small pieces of colored felt, yarn or sequins to add fingernails, rings, and other decorations to coin holder.

Dad can place his pocket change and keys on the coin holder each night when he gets ready for bed. In the morning, he will know right where to find the things he needs.

Strawberry Potholder Gift!

Mom will love receiving this handmade potholder!

Cut two strawberry patterns from red felt. Cut the stem from a folded piece of green felt. Stitch or glue the edges of the strawberry together. Glue the stem to the top, as shown. (The loop in the stem will form a convenient handle.) Children may like to cross-stitch a few designs on the face of the potholder as decoration.

Rudolph!

Color and cut out this Rudolph pattern from brown paper.

Have each student trace both of their hands onto brown construction paper and cut them out. Instruct them to glue the hands (antlers) to the top of his head, as shown.
A red, round nose can also be glued into place.

Display Rudolph on the class door or bulletin board.

My Hanukkah Book!

Matching Candles!

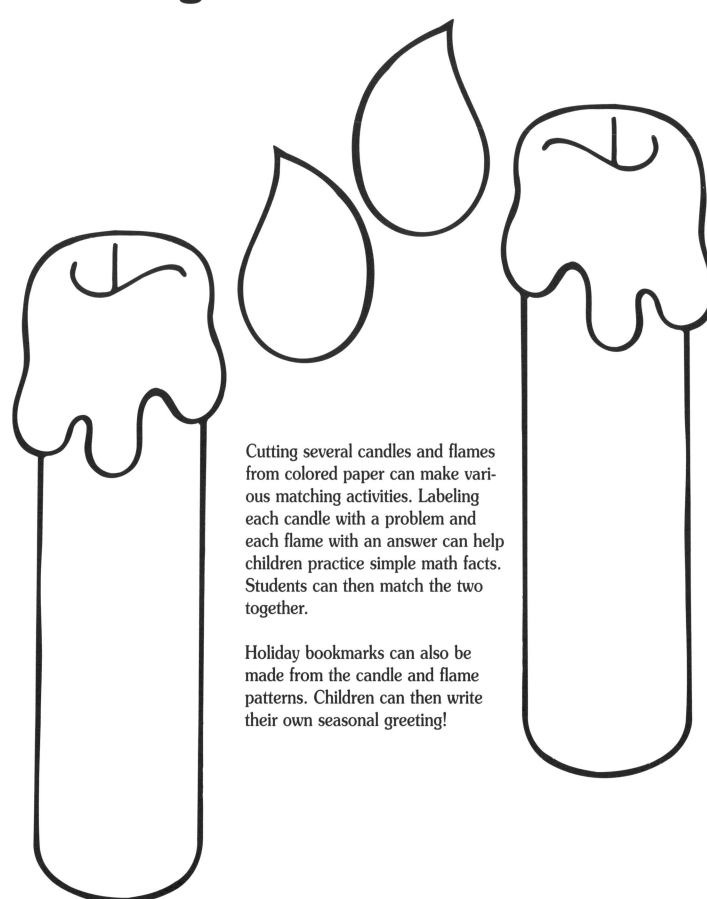

Cutting several candles and flames from colored paper can make various matching activities. Labeling each candle with a problem and each flame with an answer can help children practice simple math facts. Students can then match the two together.

Holiday bookmarks can also be made from the candle and flame patterns. Children can then write their own seasonal greeting!

                                       TF1602 Winter Idea Book

JANUARY CLIP ART
JANUARY AWARDS
JANUARY ACTIVITIES
JANUARY FUN GLASSES
NEW YEAR DIARY
JANUARY BULLETIN BOARDS
TIME AWARDS
TIME CARDS
CLOCK PATTERNS
NEW YEARS RESOLUTION MOBILE

JAN
UARY

January Clip Art!

JANUARY NEWSLETTER!

TEACHER:

RM#   **DATE:**

Type the name of your school, address and telephone number in this space.

SUGGESTIONS FOR A JANUARY NEWSLETTER:

- List the name of each student that was selected student of the week for the month of December.

- Note the dates of Martin Luther King, Jr. Day. Make sure that parents know which day or days children will not be in attendance.

- Announce special programs being conducted by your school or in your classroom.

- Tell about something special on which your class is currently working.

- Ask your school principal to write a brief message that can be included with the January newsletter.

- Staple the January cafeteria menu to each newsletter.

- Announce upcoming field trips, class plays, spelling bees or fund raisers.

- Ask one of your students to draw several small pictures about the winter season, Dr. Martin Luther King, Jr. or Chinese New Year to be used as clip art.

- Send a welcome note to a new student or a get-well message to a student that has been out ill.

- Wish each of your students and their parents a happy and successful new year!

SUPER STUDENT AWARD!

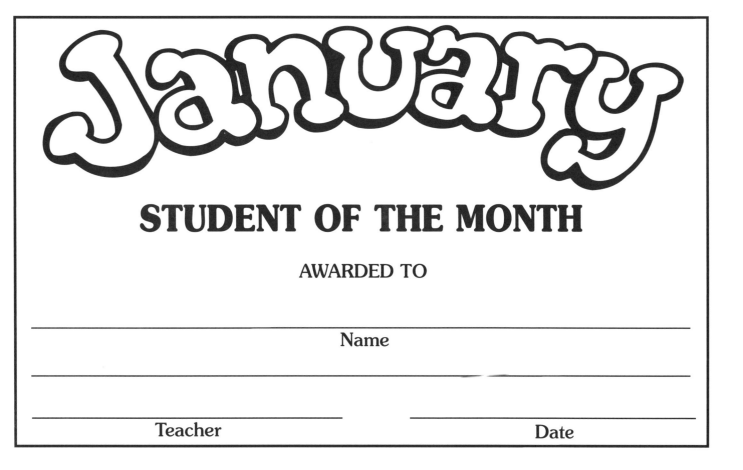

awarded to

_____

for

_____

_____

_____

_____

Date

_____

Teacher

January

STUDENT OF THE MONTH

AWARDED TO

_____

Name

_____

_____   _____

Teacher   Date

JANUARY ACTIVITIES!

JANUARY
My new calendar is temporary.
Of course, it begins in January,
But when 365 days are done,
I know I'll need another one.

In January, cold weather stays
Every one of 31 days.
Football fans will watch and freeze.
But most stay home with their TV's.

TIME MARCHES ON
January offers the perfect opportunity to teach the concept of time. You might want to display a large clock face on the class bulletin board, or have each student make his or her own large clock face with movable hands. The teacher can call out a specific time and then instruct the students to arrange the clock hands on their individual clocks to the correct time.

With younger students, explore the concepts of past, present, future, before and after.

RESOLUTION T-SHIRTS
Students love to make statements with the clothes they wear. In this case, have that statement be a positive New Year's resolution!

Have each student bring to school a plain colored or white T-shirt. Students can design their own personal resolutions using permanent colored markers. (Place a piece of cardboard on the inside of each T-shirt prior to coloring to keep the colors from bleeding through.) You may like to display the shirts on a class clothesline before letting the students wear them.

To avoid the cost of real T-shirts, simply make paper T-shirts cut from white butcher paper. These will also make a fun, creative class display!

JANUS
In ancient times, the Romans had a god who was responsible for watching the old year go and the new year come. To do this, he is said to have had two faces so that he could look both ways at the same time. The Romans called this two-faced god Janus. Our first month, January, is named after him.

Students might like to discuss what the term "two-faced" means today. Older students can also research other Roman and Greek gods and find out about their names and legends.

MY NEW YEAR'S RESOLUTIONS!

Think about the positive things you could do to improve the world around you. Write your ideas in the spaces provided.

My Home: _____

_____

My Classroom: _____

_____

My School: _____

_____

My Community: _____

_____

The World: _____

_____

This year, I would like to... _____

_____

If I could change one thing, it would be... _____

_____

January Fun Glasses!

HAPPY NEW YEAR!

CUT OUT

CUT OUT

B

A

B

A

Cut the pattern pieces from heavy index paper and color with markers or crayons. Attach the bows to the frame by fitting them into the designated slots.

My
New
Year
Diary!

Name

JANUARY BULLETIN BOARDS!

Ring in a New You!

Ask students to write their New Year's resolutions or self-improvement goals on a bell pattern. These goals might include behaviors that could be accomplished at school, such as completion of all homework assignments for the next two weeks or receive a "B" or better on the next spelling test. Children could then earn stickers when the goals are reached.

Mystery Message

On a large sheet of colored butcher paper, write a mystery message in large, bold letters. Cut the paper into numerous squares and make sure each student has his or her own piece.

Ask students to arrange their pieces on the class bulletin board to solve the mystery. You can use this idea anytime during the year, simply change the message!

Make A Wish

Children can make their wishes known using a wishing well pattern. Instruct the students to write three wishes for the coming year on a wishing well. These might include a wish for peace on Earth or a solution to the drug problem. Large Lincoln pennies can also be part of the display. (See pattern on page 99.)

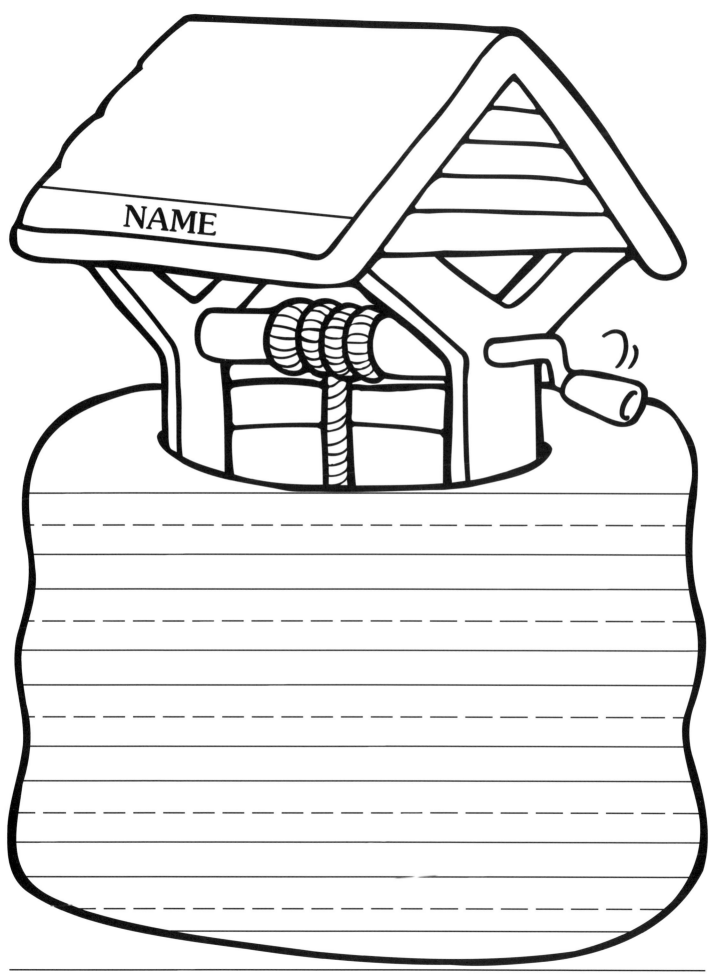

NAME

My New Year's Resolutions

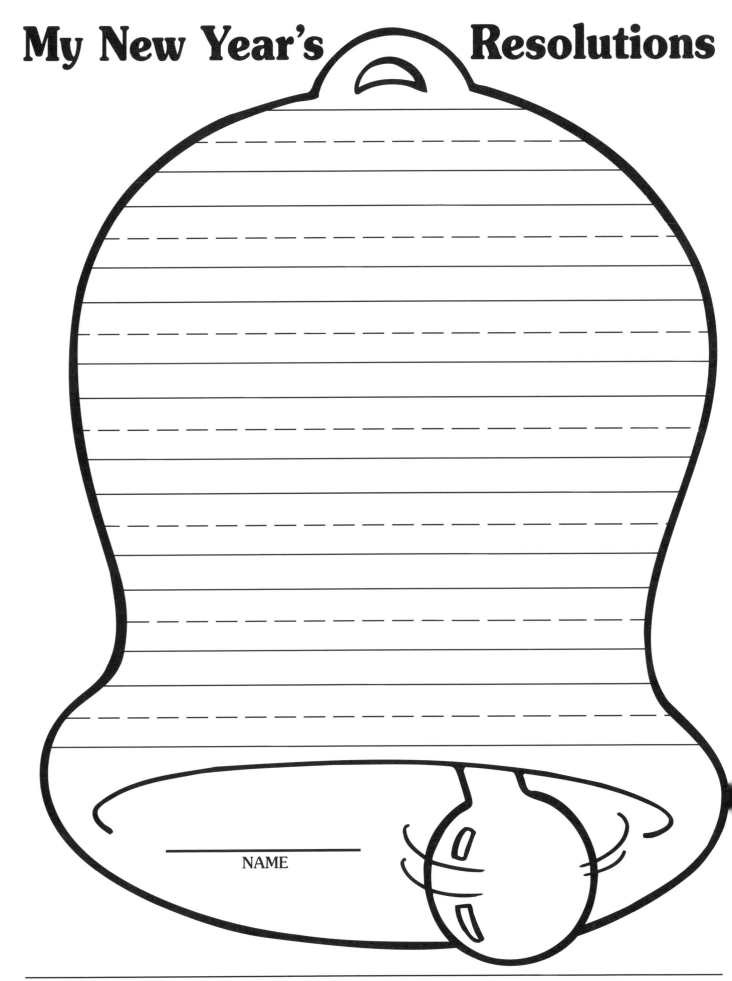

NAME

Time Awards!

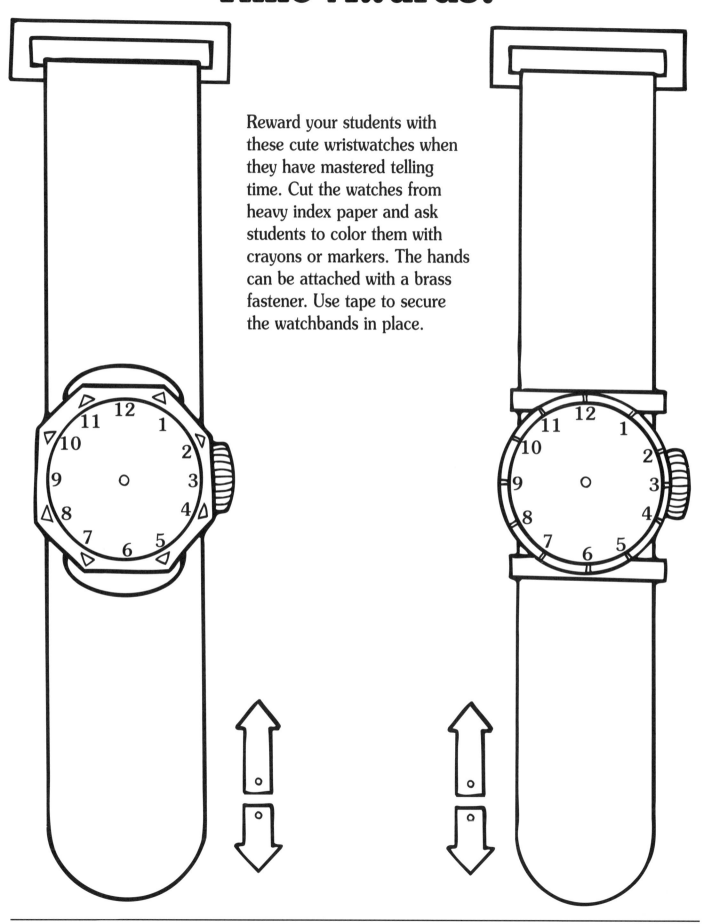

Reward your students with these cute wristwatches when they have mastered telling time. Cut the watches from heavy index paper and ask students to color them with crayons or markers. The hands can be attached with a brass fastener. Use tape to secure the watchbands in place.

Clock Pattern!

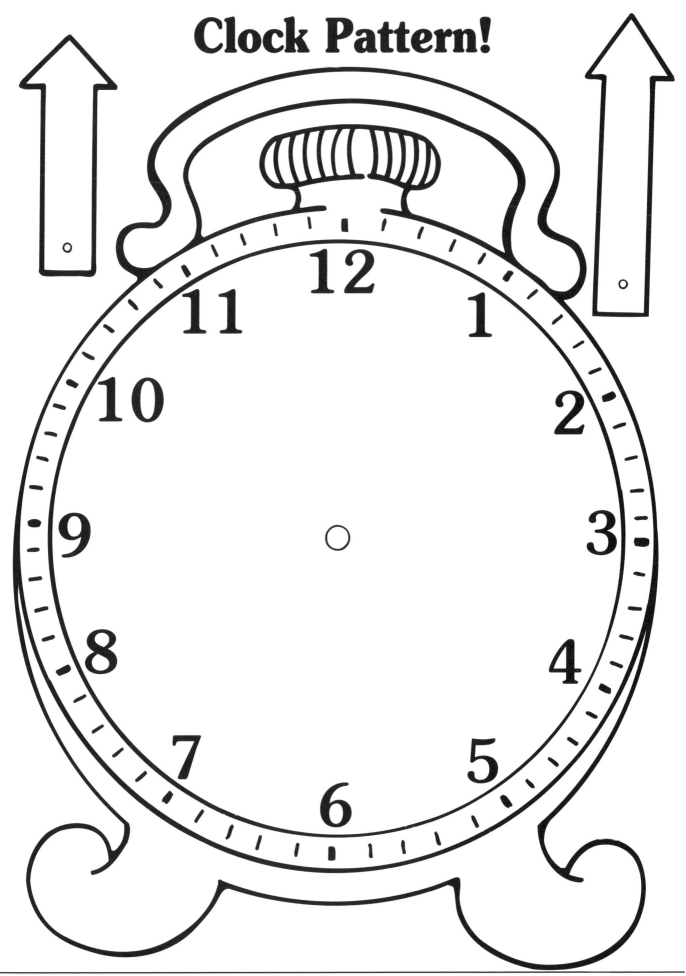

Reinforce the concept of time by using these blank clock faces. Make several copies and draw in your own clock hands. Children can match each clock with the correct time cards, found on the next pages.

12:20	**4:15**
7:35	**3:50**
6:45	**1:05**
1:25	**2:30**

5:10	**3:15**
12:45	**7:20**
1:40	**9:30**
8:40	**6:55**

New Year's Resolution Mobile!

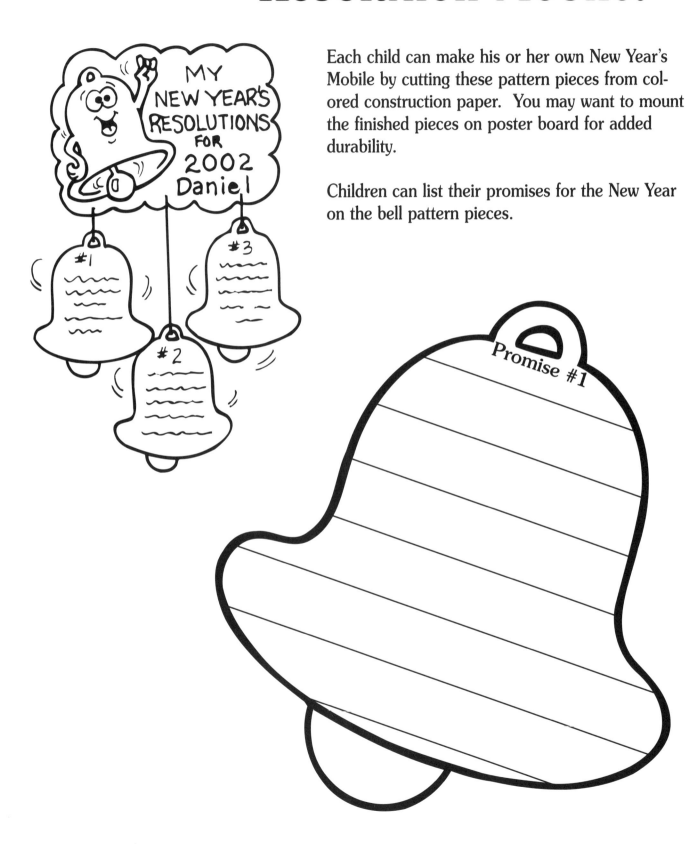

Each child can make his or her own New Year's Mobile by cutting these pattern pieces from colored construction paper. You may want to mount the finished pieces on poster board for added durability.

Children can list their promises for the New Year on the bell pattern pieces.

My New Year's Resolutions

For

Year

Name

TF1602 Winter Idea Book

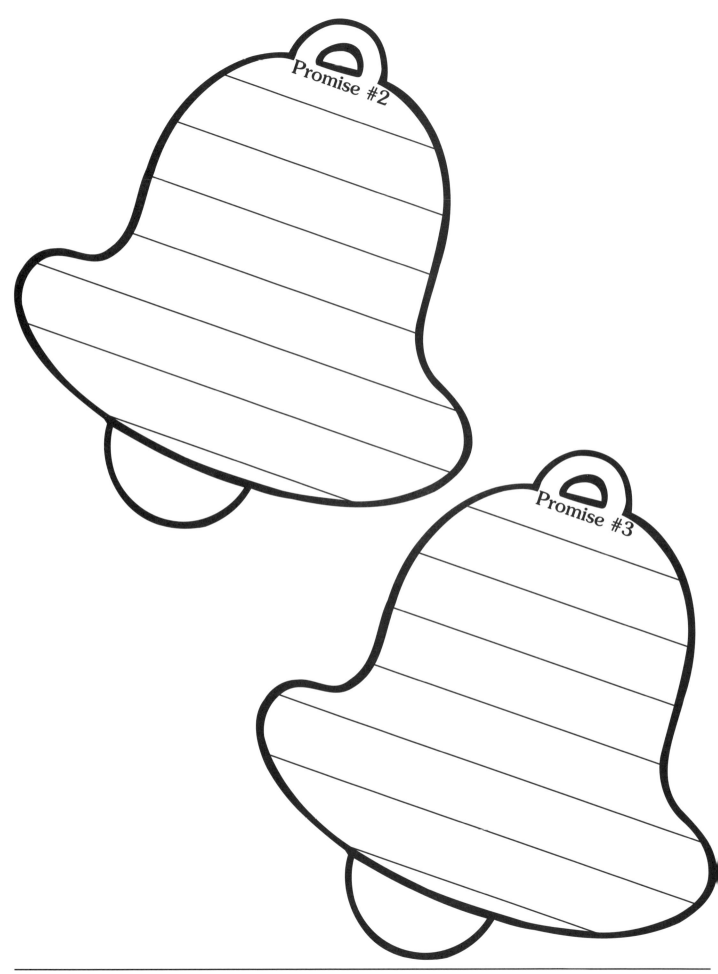

Promise #2

Promise #3

FEBRUARY CLIP ART
FEBRUARY AWARDS
FEBRUARY ACTIVITIES
FEBRUARY BULLETIN BOARDS
FEBRUARY FUN GLASSES
VALENTINE CRAFTS
BLACK HISTORY ACTIVITIES

LINCOLN CHARACTER
WASHINGTON CHARACTER
PRESIDENTS' DAY GAME
LINCOLN & WASHINGTON MOBILE
WASHINGTON DOLLAR
LINCOLN PENNY
CONTRIBUTION PATTERNS

TF1602 Winter Idea Book

February Clip Art

FEBRUARY NEWSLETTER!

TEACHER:

RM#   **DATE:**

Type the name of your
school, address and
telephone number
in this space.

SUGGESTIONS FOR A FEBRUARY NEWSLETTER:

- List the name of each student that was selected student of the week for the month of January.

- Note the dates of Washington's and Lincoln's birthdays. Make sure that parents know which days children will not be in attendance.

- Announce special programs or parties being conducted by your school or in your classroom.

- Ask for parent volunteers or donations for the class Valentine's Day party.

- Ask one of your students to draw several small pictures about Valentine's Day or Presidents' Day.

- Ask your school principal to write a brief message that can be included with the February newsletter.

- Staple the February cafeteria menu to each newsletter.

- Send a welcome note to a new student or a get-well message to a student that has been out ill.

- This month starts a new semester in the school year. Include a list of your classroom goals for your students' parents. If your school schedules parent conferences during this month, remind them of the dates.

- Announce upcoming field trips, class plays, spelling bees or fund raisers.

SUPER STUDENT AWARD!

awarded to

_____

for

_____

_____

_____

_____

Date

_____

Teacher

February

STUDENT OF THE MONTH

AWARDED TO

_____

Name

_____

_____   _____

Teacher   Date

FEBRUARY ACTIVITIES!

FEBRUARY'S EXTRA DAY

Every four years as planets rotate,
Our calendar needs another date.
Add one to February—that's fine,
So February has twenty-nine.
Leap Year Day then appears
Only once every four years.
And on the this day in February
A girl may ask a boy to marry.
All other days, I suppose,
Boys are encouraged to propose.

ABE'S LEGS

Abe Lincoln always had long legs,
A very tall man was he.
Someone asked him how long he thought
A man's legs ought to be.

He answered quick
With look profound,
"Long enough
To reach the ground!"

FAMOUS NAMES

Everything from states and cities to streets and
schools have been named after George
Washington and Abraham Lincoln. Ask students to
list as many places and things named after the two
presidents as they can. Make sure that they
consider local, as well as national and
international places. Ask the students to locate
these places on the classroom map.

LINCOLN AND WASHINGTON

Washington and Lincoln, as well as many other
famous Americans, appear on our country's coins,
bills and postage stamps. Ask students to find out
the history of the Lincoln penny and the
Washington dollar bill.

FEBRUARY BULLETIN BOARDS

LINCOLN AND WASHINGTON

Display a large dollar bill and a Lincoln penny on the class bulletin board. Have students list various facts about both presidents or give them historical math problems that can be listed on the board. Some questions might be: If Washington was still alive today, how old would he be? How many years did the Civil War last?

VALENTINE WISHES

Using pink and red construction paper, have each student cut two large heart shapes. Ask each student to write his or her name on one heart and a valentine wish for the world on the other. Arrange the hearts in a giant heart shape on the class bulletin board.

BLACK HISTORY MONTH

Create an extra large matching activity using the names of famous Black Americans and their individual contributions. Students can use pieces of yarn to connect the name with the correct accomplishment.

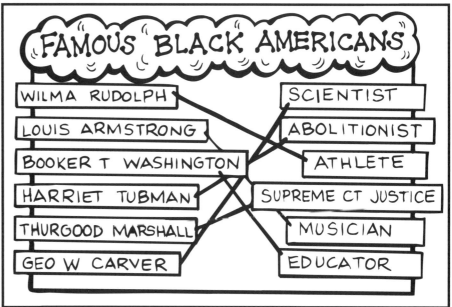

Stand-Up Valentines!

Cut out this row of hearts from heavy paper. Write your own valentine message on the hearts. Fan-fold along the dotted lines. Glue the larger valentine to the first heart and stand the valentine on a desk top for a Valentine's Day decoration.

February Fun Glasses!

Cut the pattern pieces from heavy index paper and color with markers or crayons. Attach the bows to the frame by fitting them into the designated slots.

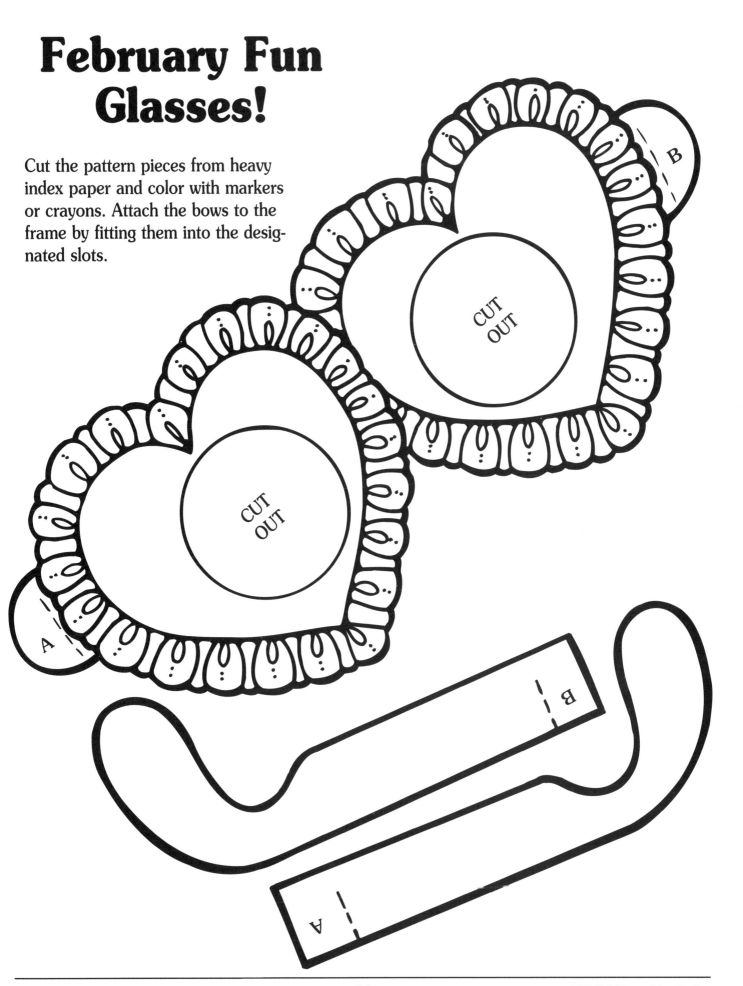

Valentine Frame!

This simple valentine frame makes a wonderful February craft or a great gift for mom or dad.

Copy the pattern to a piece of folded index or construction paper. Cut out the inside of the heart shape and glue a child's photo inside the folded half. A
simple stand can be made by stapling the discarded heart shape to the back of the frame, as shown.

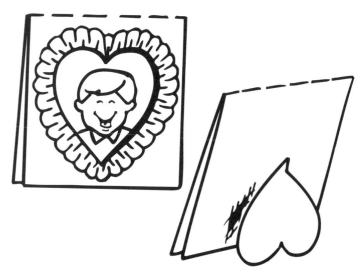

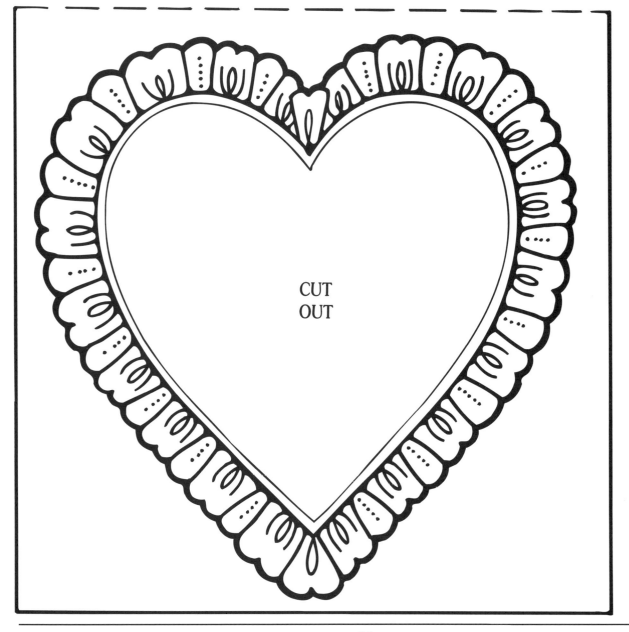

CUT
OUT

Woven Valentine!

Cutting two patterns, one from red paper and one from white, easily makes this woven valentine. Fold the pattern in half and make three cuts up the center.

Hold one pattern in each hand. Carefully weave the first loop of the piece in your right hand under and over the piece in your left hand. Weave each of the loops in the same way.

When completed, it will look like a checkered heart, as shown. Staple a handle to the top of the woven valentine and fill it with wrapped candy.

You might like to enlarge the pattern and make an extra large woven valentine. It could be used to hold all of the valentines you collect on February 14th.

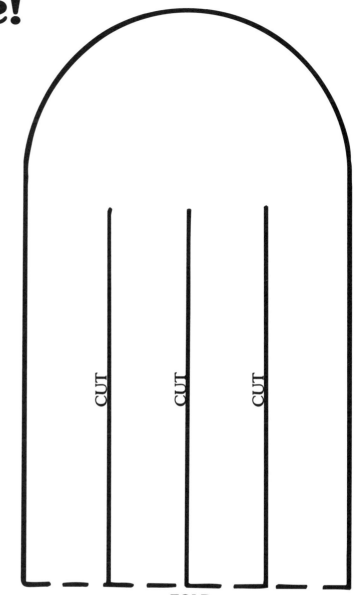

CUT   CUT   CUT

FOLD

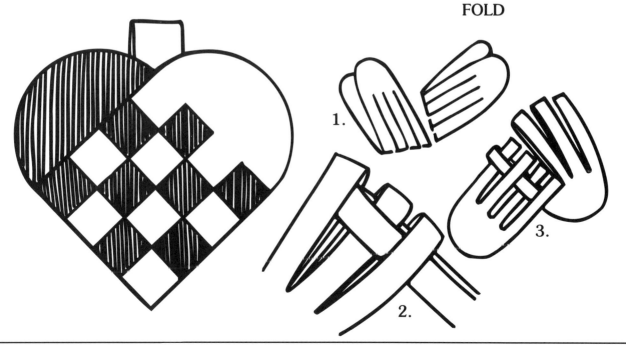

1.

2.

3.

Valentine Tales!

Matching Heart Halves!

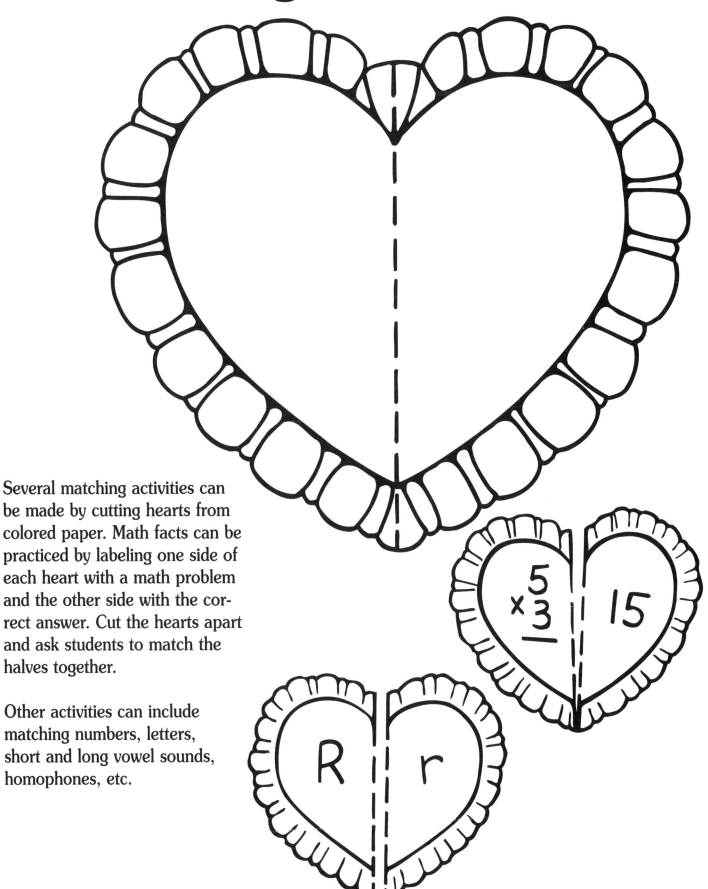

Several matching activities can be made by cutting hearts from colored paper. Math facts can be practiced by labeling one side of each heart with a math problem and the other side with the correct answer. Cut the hearts apart and ask students to match the halves together.

Other activities can include matching numbers, letters, short and long vowel sounds, homophones, etc.

$$\begin{array}{r} 5 \\ \times\ 3 \\ \hline \end{array}$$

15

R r

TF1602 Winter Idea Book

BLACK HISTORY ACTIVITIES!

Ask each student to research and write about one Black American who has contributed greatly in one or more of the following areas:

Education   Science
Politics   Literature
Athletics   Business
Entertainment   Medicine

BLACK HISTORY RESEARCH

Have each student choose a famous Black American to research from the list below. Encourage them to draw a portrait of the person they have chosen. The drawings can be displayed with the individual reports.

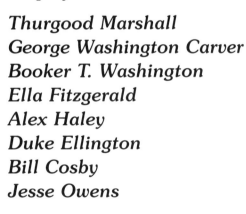

Thurgood Marshall
George Washington Carver
Booker T. Washington
Ella Fitzgerald
Alex Haley
Duke Ellington
Bill Cosby
Jesse Owens

Langston Hughes
Martin Luther King, Jr.
Oprah Winfrey
Jesse Jackson
Harriet Tubman
Frederick Douglass
Rosa Parks
Hank Aaron

Crispus Attucks
Louis Armstrong
Mary McLeod Bethune
Wilma Rudolph
Charles Richard Drew
Muhammad Ali
Ralph Abernathy

MUSICAL FEELINGS

Play the music of several Black artists. If possible, introduce jazz and black gospel music to your students. Ask them to write about their moods or feelings while listening to the music.

CLASS DISCUSSIONS

Ask your students to discuss the following words:
Freedom   Liberty   Brotherhood   Prejudice

Students might like to illustrate one of these terms and display the drawings on the class bulletin board.

A FAMOUS BLACK AMERICAN

Contribution Patterns!

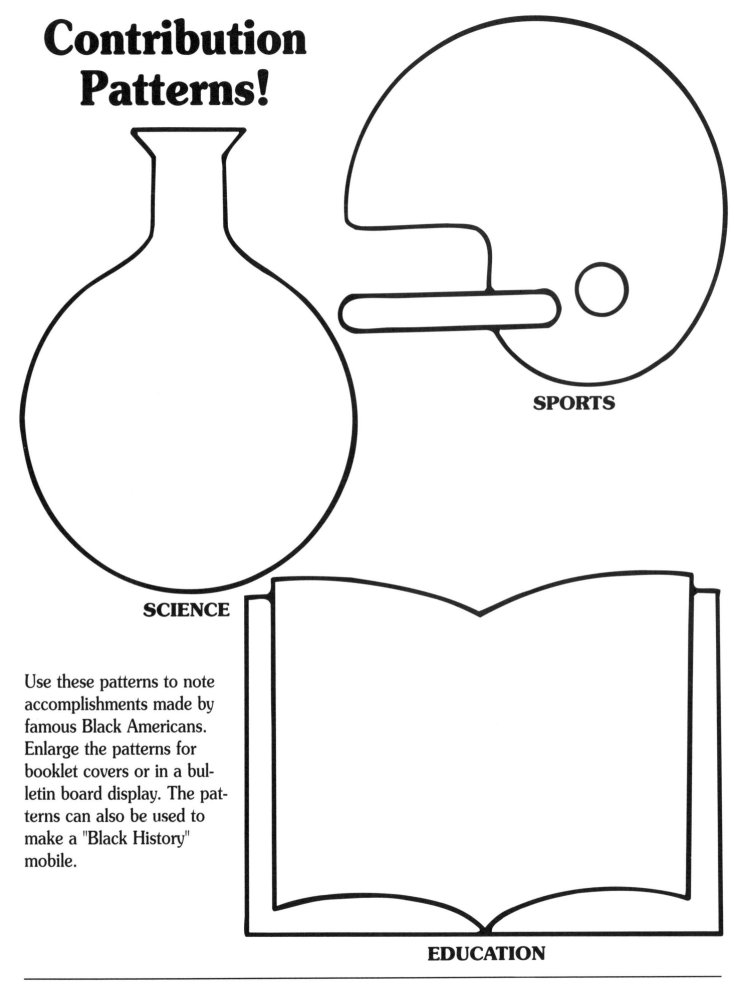

SPORTS

SCIENCE

Use these patterns to note accomplishments made by famous Black Americans. Enlarge the patterns for booklet covers or in a bulletin board display. The patterns can also be used to make a "Black History" mobile.

EDUCATION

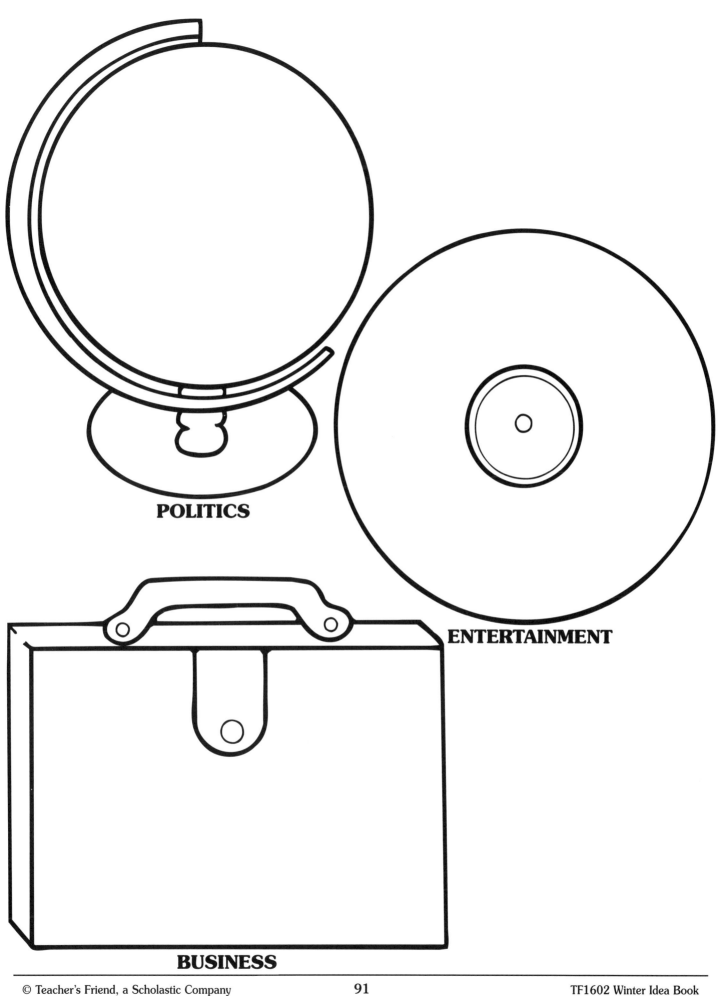

POLITICS

ENTERTAINMENT

BUSINESS

 TF1602 Winter Idea Book

Lincoln Character!

Make this Abraham Lincoln character from index or construction paper. Color, cut and fold. Attach the scroll to his right hand. Stand him on a tabletop to celebrate the president's birthday.

Washington Character!

Make this George Washington character from index paper. Color, cut and fold. Attach the hatchet to his right hand. Stand him on a tabletop to celebrate Washington's birthday.

PRESIDENTS'

START

1.
2.
3.
14.
13.
12.
4.
11.
5.
LINCOLN
10.
6.
9.
7.
8.

TF1602 Winter Idea Book

DAY GAME!

Make your own task cards for this game that two, three or four children can play.

27. 28.

FINISH

26.

15.

16.

17.

25.

18.

WASHINGTON

24.

19.

23.

20.

22.

21.

Lincoln & Washington Mobile!

Each student can make his or her own Lincoln and Washington Mobile by cutting these pattern pieces from colored construction paper. Patterns can also be used as nametags or calendar decorations.

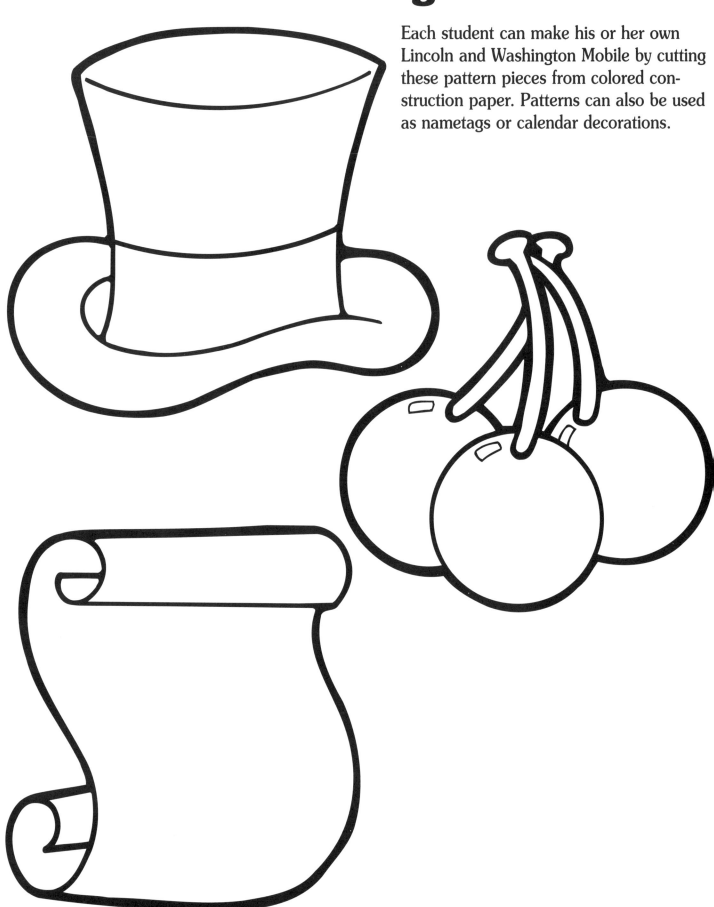

Washington Dollar!

Award paper "dollars" to students that accomplish specific tasks or improve behavior. On the last day of the week, let students trade in their dollars for a small prize or free time in the classroom.

Lincoln Penny!

Use this Lincoln Penny pattern for a booklet cover or to make a bulletin board display. Copy the pattern onto "copper" colored construction paper.

MY PRESIDENTS REPORT!

BASKETBALL ACTIVITIES
BASKETBALL CHARACTER
SHOOT FOR THE HOOP GAME
CREATIVE WRITING BASKETBALLS
BASKETBALL BULLETIN BOARDS
MY BASKETBALL BOOK

BASKETBALL ACTIVITIES!

BASKETBALL HEIGHTS

You have to be especially tall
To qualify for basketball.
All players are, of course, quite strong.
Their legs and arms are extra long.
The ball is dribbled on the floor,
Thrown through the basket for a score.
I love to watch this lively sport
But, rather be playing on the court.
This game has been my great desire
If only I'd grown inches higher.
Did you ever hear of a team or sport
Just for people who are short?

RAINY DAY BASKETBALL

Break the winter doldrums with this simple rainy day activity.

Divide the class into two teams. Have each team player shoot free shots into a wastebasket using a crumpled piece of paper or a lightweight foam rubber ball. Keep score and award the winning team an extra five minutes of free time.

You may want students to practice specific facts, such as spelling words or multiplication tables, before they are permitted to shoot for a basket.

BASKETBALL BINGO!

This game offers an exciting way to introduce students to basketball. Give each child a copy of the bingo words listed below or write the words on the chalkboard. Ask students to write any 24 words on his or her bingo card. Use the same directions you might use for regular bingo.

BASKETBALL	FREE THROW	GUARD	COACH
COURT	CENTER	JUMP SHOT	BASKET
TEAM	FORWARD	BASKET	PENALTY
SCORE	BACK COURT	OUT OF BOUNDS	SHOT
OFFICIAL	FRONT COURT	FOUL	BENCH
REFEREE	DRIBBLING	SHOOT	NET
UMPIRE	LAY UP	SLAM DUNK	PASS
OFFENSE	HOLDING	HALFTIME	BOUNCE
DEFENSE	HOOK SHOT	HOOP	TIME CLOCK
ZONE	CHARGING	BACKBOARD	GYMNASIUM

BASKETBALL BINGO

FREE

Match the Basket and Basketball

Cutting several baskets and basketballs from colored paper can make a variety of matching activities. Math facts can then be practiced by labeling each ball with a problem and a basket with the correct answer. Students solve the problem and match the two together.

9

14 - 5 =

18

3 × 6 =

Basketball Character

Make this Basketball Character from index paper. Color, cut, fold and attach the basketball to his right hand.

Stand several players on a tabletop and pretend to play your own championship game.

Shoot for the Hoop!

2.

3.

1.

4.

5.

6.

Teacher: Two, three or four children can play this game. Make your own task cards or write a math problem that must be solved on each basketball.

7.

8.

9.

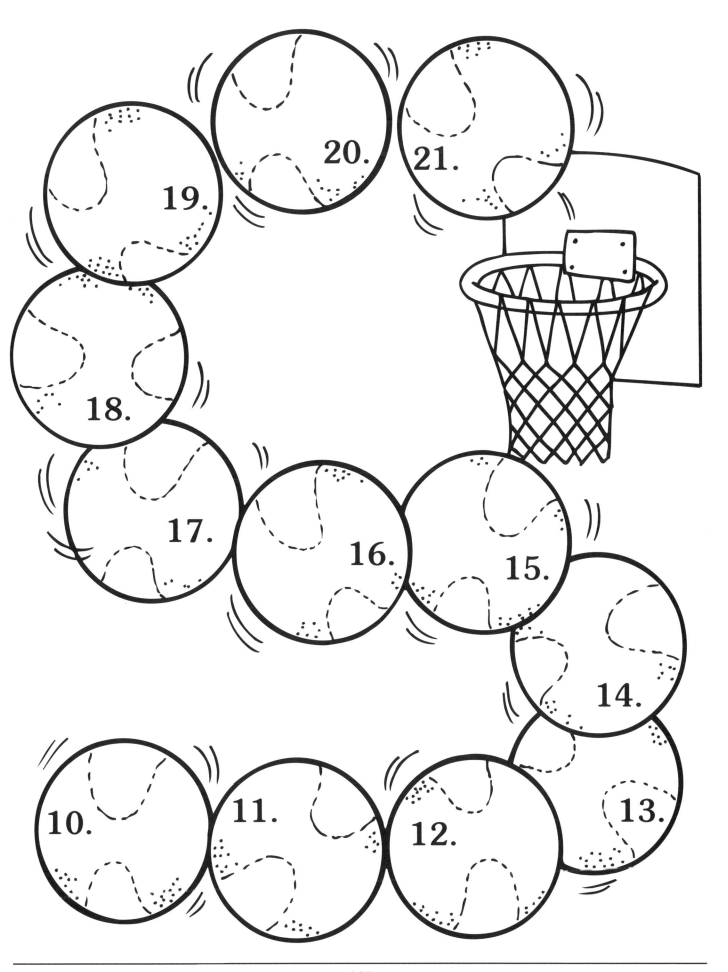

Creative Writing Basketballs!

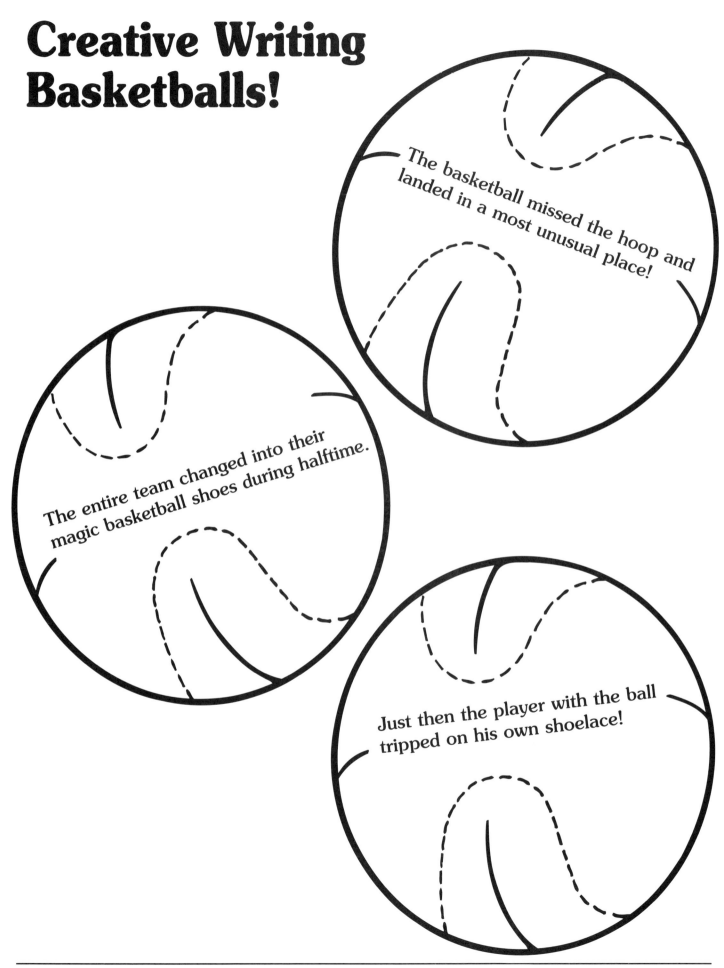

The basketball missed the hoop and landed in a most unusual place!

The entire team changed into their magic basketball shoes during halftime.

Just then the player with the ball tripped on his own shoelace!

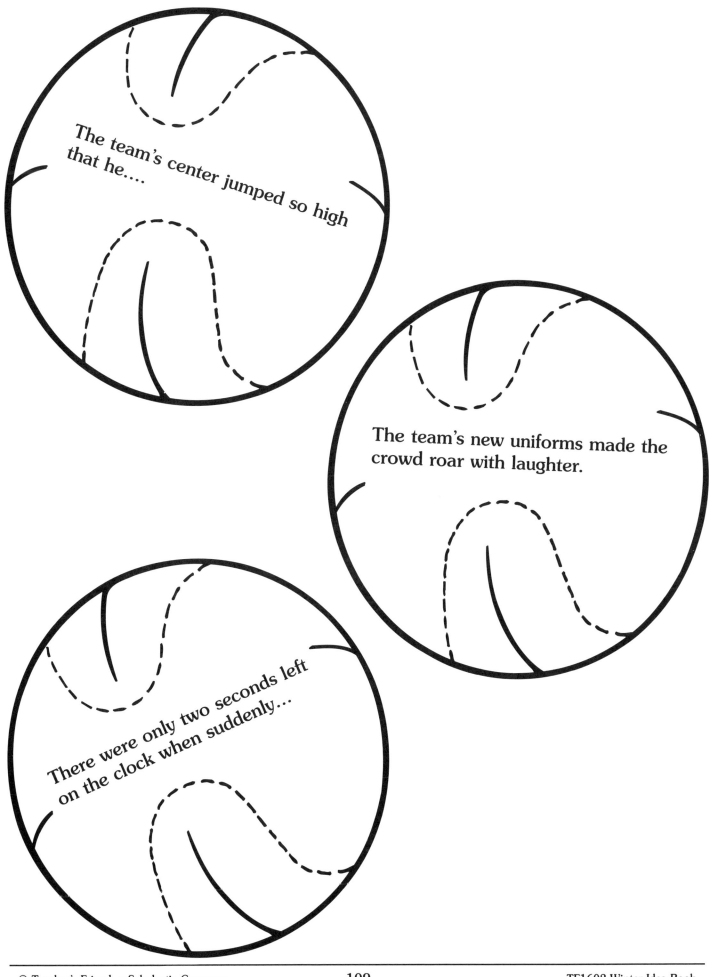

The team's center jumped so high that he....

The team's new uniforms made the crowd roar with laughter.

There were only two seconds left on the clock when suddenly...

BASKETBALL BULLETIN BOARDS!

SHOOT FOR EXCELLENCE!
Display a large basket, basketball and
pair of hands for this motivating bulletin board. You may wish to display good
work papers in and around the basketball hoop.

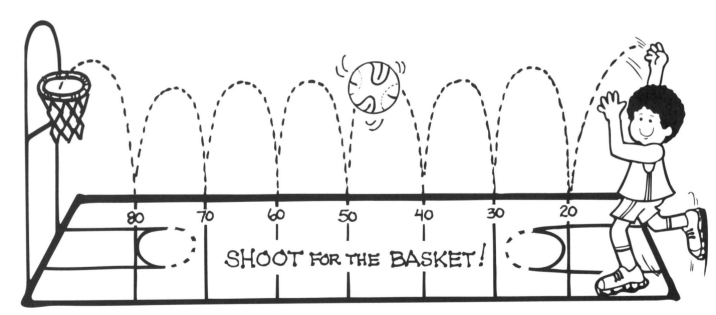

SHOOT FOR THE BASKET!
Monitor classroom goals or fund raisers with this basketball bulletin board.
Display a basketball court on the board with a basket at one end and a player
at the other. Mark the court to indicate the various goals to be accomplished.
"Bounce" the basketball down the field as your students collect points in the
contest.

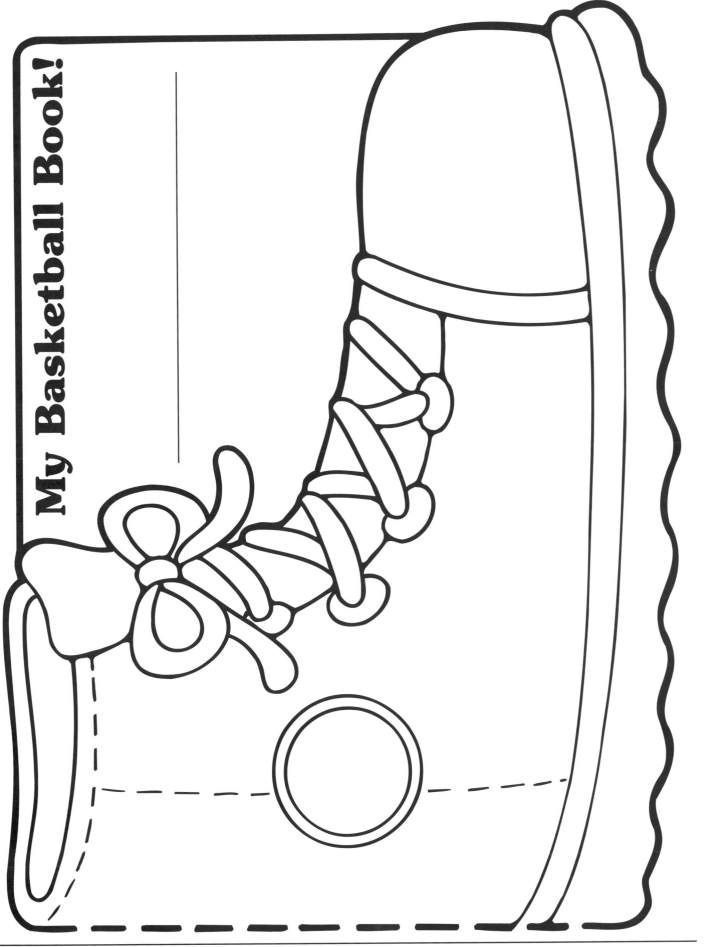

My Basketball Book!

Basketball Player!